Garment Patterns for the E[...]

by Mrs. F. E. Thompso[...]

edited by Jules & Kaethe Kliot

Originally published as *LA MODE UNIVERSELLE No.22, A Book of Pattern Designs with Thompson's Universal System of Garment Cutting*, published by Mrs. F. E. Thompson, 1905, this collection of everyday garments with basic patterns and instructions was offered to the seamstress.

The method of drafting offered was the *New and Improved* simplified layout and cutting system, developed by the author which required the use of two scales called the *Compound Scale*, to trans-late these diagrams to full size patterns.

As demonstrated by the illustrated fashions and associated patterns, the garments of this period were more of an assemblage of parts rather then a singular element. These designs should be considered only as examples of the endless possibilities using the patterns offered.

This volume should serve as a valuable resource to costume designers, pattern makers, historians and students of fashion.

LACIS PUBLICATIONS

3163 Adeline Street, Berkeley, CA 94703

© 1991, Jules Kliot, Reprint 2003

ISBN 0-916896-35-8

Instructions for Making a Pattern

The following instructions are for drafting patterns for all waists, jackets, coats, and gored skirts for both ladies and misses; also for sleeves.

LENGTH OF WAIST.

LADIES.		MISSES.	
Inches.	*Scale.*	*Inches.*	*Scale.*
11	20	8	13
11½	21	8½	14–15
12	22–23	9	16
12½	24	9½	17
13	25	10	18
13½	26–27	10½	19–20
14	28	11	21
14½	29	11½	22
15	30	12	23–24
15½	31–32	12½	25
16	33	13	26
16½	34	13½	27–28
17	35	14	29
17½	36–37	14½	30
18	38	15	31
18½	39	15½	32–33
19	40–41	16	34
19½	42	16½	35
20	43	17	36–37

TABLES OF FIGURES

LENGTH OF GORED SKIRT.

LADIES.		MISSES.	
Inches.	*Scale.*	*Inches.*	*Scale.*
28	21	15	12
29	22	16	13
30	23	17	15
31	24	18	16
32	25	19	17
33	26	20	18
34	27	21	19
35	28	22	21
36	29	23	22
37	30	24	23
38	31	25	25
39	32	26	26
40	33	27	27
41	34	28	28
42	35	29	29–30
43	36	30	31
44	37	31	32
45	38	32	33
46	39	33	34–35
47	40	34	36
48	41	35	37
		36	38
		37	39
		38	40

LENGTH OF SLEEVE.

LADIES AND MISSES.

Inches.	Scale.
10	17
10½	18
11	19
11½	20
12	21–22
12½	23
13	24
13½	25
14	26
14½	27–28
15	29
15½	30
16	31–32
16½	33
17	34
17½	35
18	36
18½	37–38
19	39
19½	40
20	41
20½	42–43
21	44
21½	45
22	46
22½	47–48
23	49
23½	50

This is an improved method, saving much time and labor, and making much more perfect patterns. While the old instructions are left unchanged, the beginner can master the system by learning the following. The old instructions may be used for reference whenever needed.

First take a measurement of the bust and the length of back from neck to waist-line. We will say that the bust measurement is 34 inches and the length of back is 16 inches.

Select Scale 34, the same number as the inches in bust measurement. Refer to the table of figures for "Length of Waist," where you will learn that when the waist is 16 inches you are to use Scale 33. Take out Scale 33.

Seat yourself at a table with paper and tools and the two scales, 34 and 33, and draft the plain basque back in the diagram below.

Lay the square on the paper with the short end to the right, thus: ⌐, and draw a line down the side nearest you, and up the short end. These form the "base-lines" from which all measurements are to be made.

Now take Scale 33 (which is the scale in this instance that is to regulate the *length* of this garment), and measure with it down the base-line nearest you, beginning at the right hand corner (where the lines join), measuring to the left. Make a mark at each point indicated by the figures on the diagram.

For instance, ½ means one-half space from the point of beginning—make a mark there; 2½ means two and one-half spaces from point of beginning—make a mark there, and so on. At the end of the scale, 10 spaces, make a mark, thus: +, as shown in the diagram. Move down the scale one length, and continue marking the points indicated by the figures in the diagram. These points are for the cross lines.

Next, place the square accurately on the base-line on which you have been making points, and draw a straight line across at every point, as shown in the diagram.

Now take the scale that corresponds with the bust measure, which in this case is 34, and make all measurements on the cross lines with that scale. At the point of ½ there is no line. On line 2½ make a mark across that line at 6 spaces from the base-line, and continue on with all the other cross lines.

With the square, now draw the straight lines of the pattern, simply copying from the diagram. Then, with the scroll, draw the curved lines. In the most important of the curved lines it is usual to have the scroll touch at three different points without changing its position—like the line in this diagram running from the armhole down to the waist.

This operation of measurement applies to every other part of every pattern or diagram for the entire System. It *is* the System.

But the two scales, called Compound Scale, are not used except on waists, jackets, and sleeves for ladies and misses, and gored skirts for ladies and misses. All other patterns are drafted by one scale only—according to directions in general instructions under the heading "What Scale to Use."

For drafting patterns for sleeves by the Compound Scale, take the measurement of arm, as for any long sleeve, with tape-line, and select a scale by the table of figures given. Make the points for the length of the sleeve by this scale, but use the bust-measure scale for the points on all cross lines.

Some patterns are given especially for "stout or fleshy ladies." These are to be drafted altogether by the scale corresponding with bust measurement.

The following tables will show what scale to use in making patterns for waists, jackets, coats, sleeves, and gored skirts for ladies and misses, to regulate the length without changes:

PATTERN KEY TO ILUSTRATIONS

N/A indicates pattern not available

34

35

See PATTERN KEY TO ILLUSTRATIONS, pages 3 and 4 for page number on which patterns may be found.

34

35

See PATTERN KEY TO ILLUSTRATIONS, pages 3 and 4 for page number on which patterns may be found.

See PATTERN KEY TO ILLUSTRATIONS, pages 3 and 4 for page number on which patterns may be found.

See PATTERN KEY TO ILLUSTRATIONS, pages 3 and 4 for page number on which patterns may be found.

57

60

61

62

58

59

See PATTERN KEY TO ILLUSTRATIONS, pages 3 and 4 for page number on which patterns may be found.

9

See PATTERN KEY TO ILLUSTRATIONS, pages 3 and 4 for page number on which patterns may be found.

See PATTERN KEY TO ILLUSTRATIONS, pages 3 and 4 for page number on which patterns may be found.

11

See PATTERN KEY TO ILLUSTRATIONS, pages 3 and 4 for page number on which patterns may be found.

See PATTERN KEY TO ILLUSTRATIONS, pages 3 and 4 for page number on which patterns may be found.

See PATTERN KEY TO ILLUSTRATIONS, pages 3 and 4 for page number on which patterns may be found.

101 102 103 104 106 107 108 109 110 111 112

See PATTERN KEY TO ILLUSTRATIONS, pages 3 and 4 for page number on which patterns may be found.

See PATTERN KEY TO ILLUSTRATIONS, pages 3 and 4 for page number on which patterns may be found.

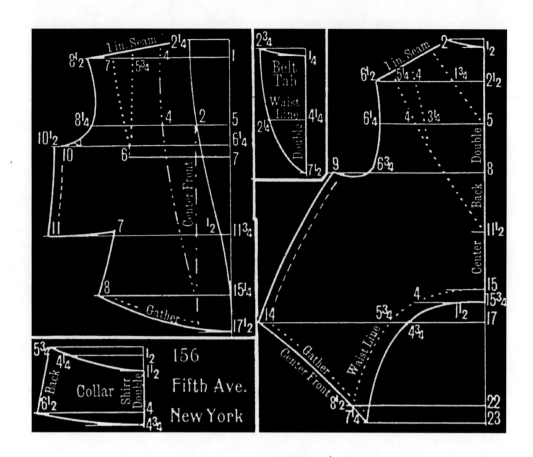

LADIES' COSTUME.

The illustration of the costume provided for on this page and the two pages following is of striking originality, most effective in design, and without an overabundance of ornamentation like so many designs which fill the pages of the fashion books at this time. There is a three-piece skirt, a bodice with girdle effect in front. The bodice is worn with a chemisette. If cut with the seam in the back, as shown in the illustration, trace on the long dotted line in diagram for back, and allow for seams. The front of the girdle effect is marked "belt tab" in the diagram, and is overlaid with upturned pleats. The handsome illustration and the minute details in the diagrams make further directions for the waist unnecessary.

An inverted pleat in front of skirt is to be folded on the dotted lines and stitched ¼ space.

Material required for medium size, waist, 4 yards, 22 inches wide; 2¾ yards, 36 inches; 2 yards, 54 inches; skirt, 8½ yards, 22 inches; 6 yards, 36 inches; 5 yards, 54 inches.

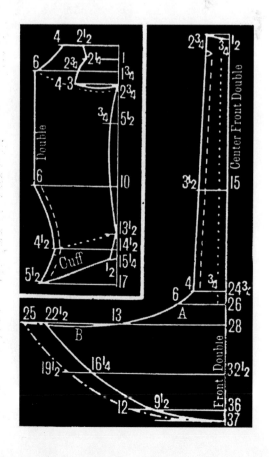

17

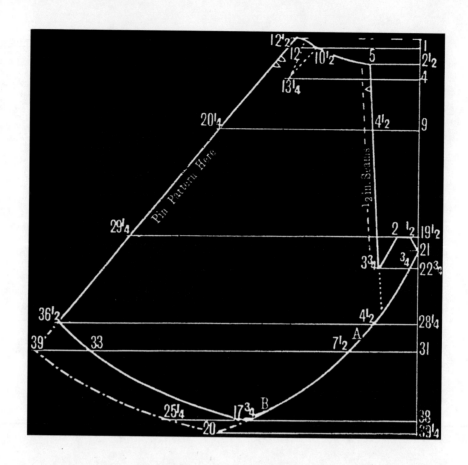

The diagrams on this page are for two sections of the skirt for ladies' costume described on the preceding page.

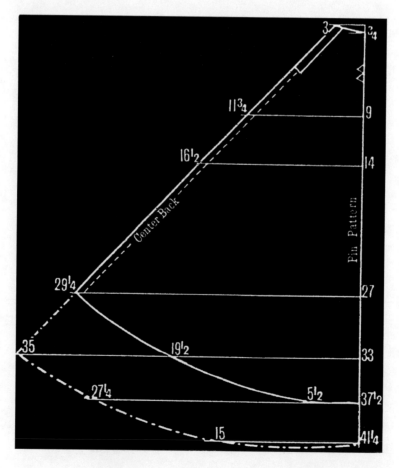

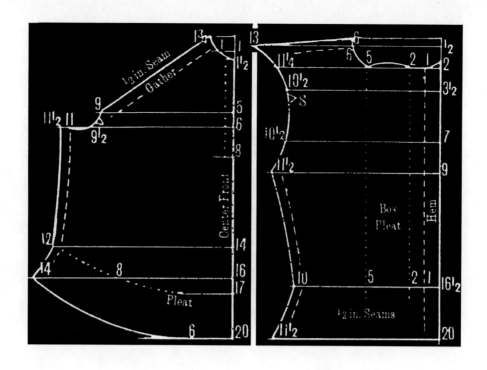

THE NEW SHIRT WAIST

The diagrams for a shirt waist and sleeve on this page are for an altogether new design strikingly attractive. The waist it made without a shoulder seam, the yoke being cut in one piece with the back of waist. It has a box pleat on each side of center back, and the closing is made under one of these. The front is shirred from the yoke on each side. The front, the collar, and cuffs are finished with a piping of like or of other material, and buttons are applied as in the illustration. The box pleats in the back are folded between the dotted lines and stitched on the lines. The cuff and sleeve are

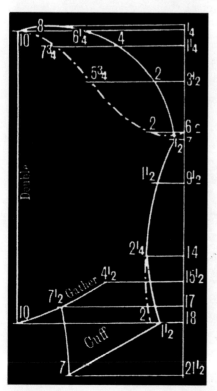

cut in one, and the sleeve is gathered into the cuff, as indicated in the diagram. The notch at "S," in diagram for back, is for top of sleeve.

Draft by Compound Scale or general instructions.

Material required for medium size, 4 yards, 22 inches wide; 3 yards, 36 inches; 2 yards, 50 inches.

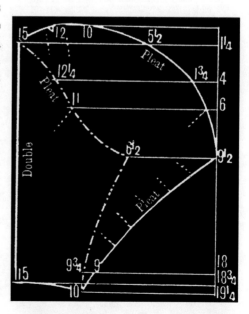

This sleeve is for the costume described on the second preceding page.

19

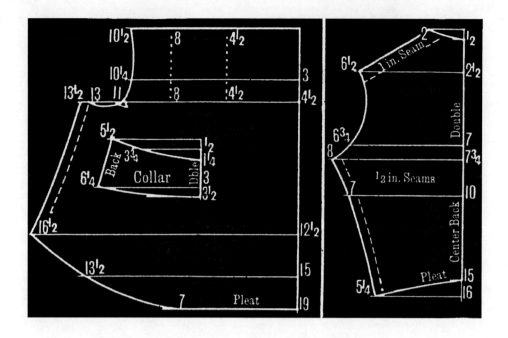

LADIES' COSTUME.

On this page and the two pages following are given diagrams for a strikingly pretty costume consisting of a surplice waist and a box-pleated skirt of handsome design. It has a very dressy sleeve, a shoulder collar trimmed with frills. From the collar to the waist are bias-stitched straps of the same material as the waist. The draped elbow sleeve has five upturned pleats applied from elbow up to the dotted line in the diagram. There is an elbow cuff. This sleeve is made over a plain sleeve, the lower part being trimmed with lace and bands of silk. The front at neck is trimmed with lace, and is worn over a vest. For fulness across the bust, fold on dotted lines of diagram and stitch 1 space deep, for two box pleats.

Draft waist and sleeve by Compound Scale.

Material required for waist, 3¾ yards, 27 inches wide; 2⅛ yards, 44 inches; 1¾ yards, 54 inches.

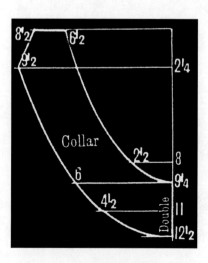

20

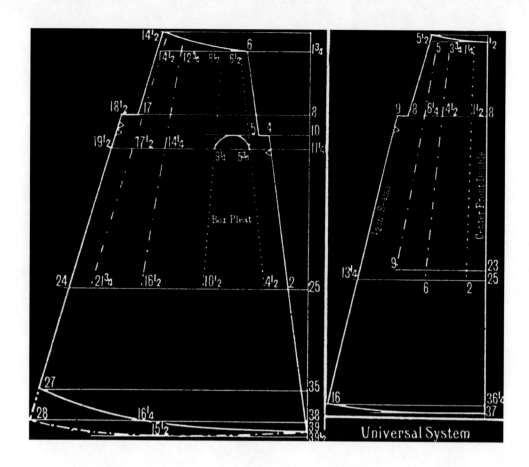

Universal System

BOX-PLEATED SKIRT.

The diagrams on this page and the following page are for the box-pleated skirt with the costume described on the preceding page. There are three box pleats on each side, with one in center front and one in center back. The illustration shows these pleats on each side cut away for insets of lace

Draft by Compound Scale.

Material required, medium size, including sweep length, 10¾ yards, 27 inches wide; 9½ yards, 44 inches; 6¾ yards, 54 inches.

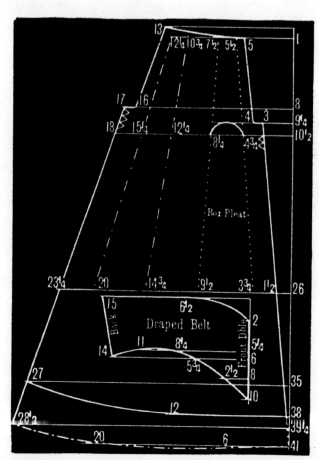

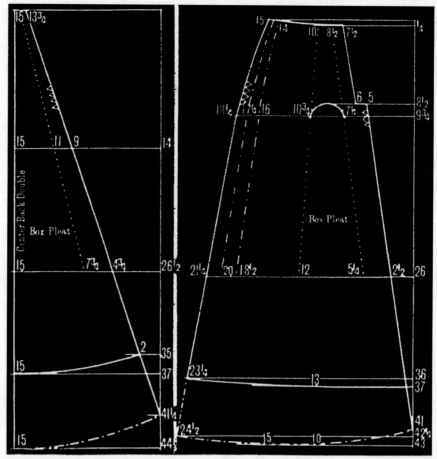

The above diagram is for the third gore and back of the box-pleated skirt described on the preceding page.

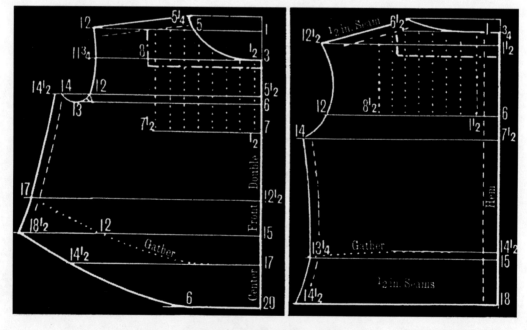

MISSES' WAIST

The diagrams above are for a misses' waist, prettily ornamented with tucks with an ornamental strap applied over the shoulders and across the front. Figures are not given for the tucks, except for the first one on back and front. The tucks are laid 1 space apart, to be folded on the lines and stitched ¼ space wide. See Explanation of Illustrations for sleeve and trimming.

Draft by Compound Scale. Material required for miss of fourteen years, 4 yards, 27 inches wide; 3 yards, 36 inches; 2 yards, 44 inches.

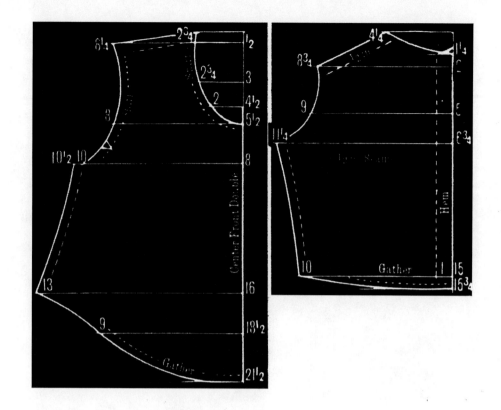

SPENCER WAIST.

A pretty spencer waist is provided for in the diagrams given here for waist and sleeve. The fulness at the neck may be either gathered or pin-tucked. The sleeve has two puffs and a ruffle. In the illustration two ruffles are given, the second one applied.

Draft by Compound Scale or general instructions.

Amount of material, 3½ yards, 22 inches wide; 2¾ yards, 27 inches; 2 yards, 44 inches.

SUSPENDER GIRDLE.

The diagram at foot of page is for a "suspender girdle." The straps are each in three pieces, cut lengthwise of material, the ends overlapping. A diagram is given for these straps, to be cut double.

Draft by scale corresponding with bust measure in inches.

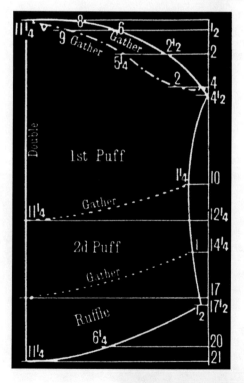

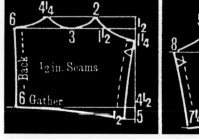

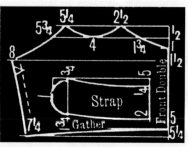

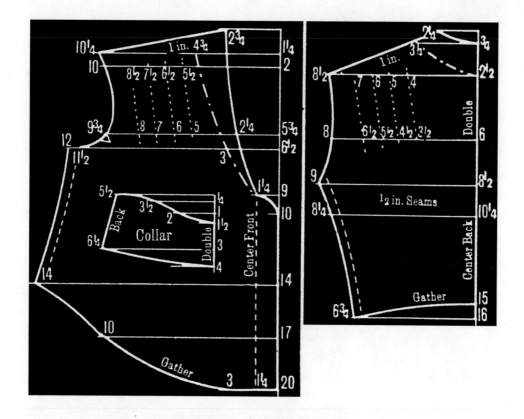

LADIES' COSTUME.

On this page and the page following are diagrams for a simple but stylish costume for ladies. It will be found to be a very useful pattern for either light or heavy materials. The chemisette may be of any other material than the lace shown in the illustration, and the ruffles of quilled ribbon may be omitted when the material would make it advisable to do so. The short sleeve is made over a plain foundation, with a puff of shirring at the elbow; the lower part of the sleeve plain, with a stitched band for a cuff, to match the trimming on the skirt. The bias straps on the skirt are 3 spaces wide when finished, and extend only across the first and second gores—leaving the back plain. The first one is 1½ spaces from bottom, and the others two spaces apart.

The diagram for waist has two lines for the front. Cut on the broken line for pattern as shown in the illustration, and on the plain line for a narrower vest. The diagram for the collar has not been properly represented by the artist, but may easily be shaped by the maker so as to be wider, like that in the illustration, if preferred.

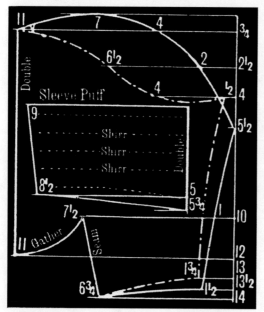

A broken line on collar diagram shows where to lay on the fold of goods for use with narrow vest.

See following page for further directions.

Material for waist, 4 yards, 22 inches wide; 2½ yards, 36 inches; 1¾ yards, 54 inches.

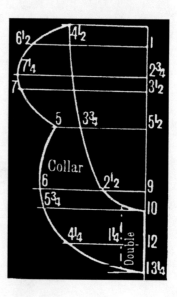

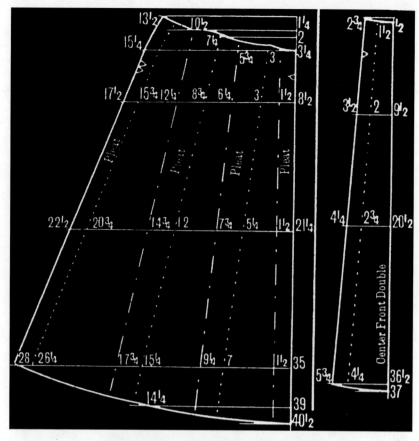

SEVEN-GORED SKIRT.

The diagrams on this page are for a seven-gored skirt designed for the ladies' costume described on the preceding page. It is a pretty and useful design for a pleated skirt. It has two box pleats in the back. The side-pleats are forward-turned. Fold on broken lines and lay over to dotted lines.

Amount of material required for medium size skirt, 8½ yards, 22 inches wide; 6½ yards, 36 inches; 4½ yards, 54 inches.

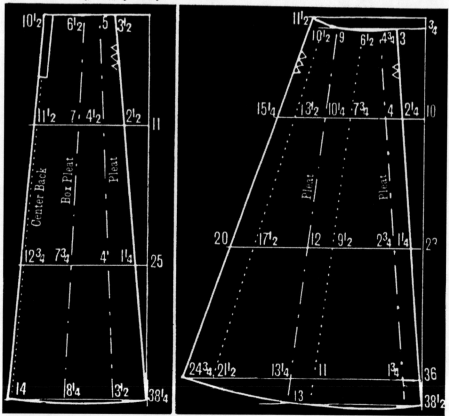

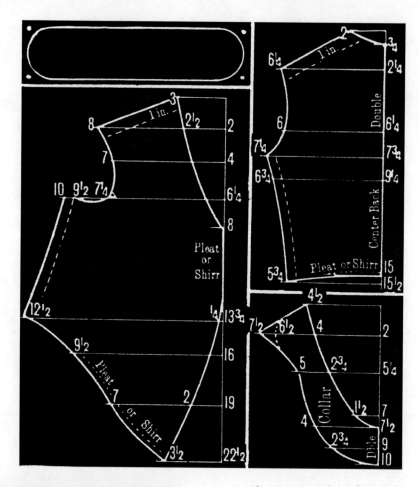

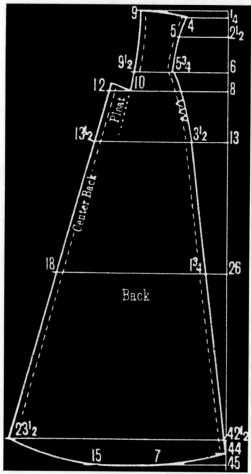

PRINCESS COSTUME.

The above diagrams with that below and those on the following page are for a princess costume which may be made as elaborate as desired by the application of trimming and ornaments. The waist is an extremely pretty design, which may be made of any material and be worn with any other skirt. As shown in the illustration the waist is trimmed with bands of lace insertion. Any other sleeve may be used in place of the elbow length.

For sleeve and directions for skirt see following page.

Material for waist, medium size, 3 yards, 22 inches wide; 2 yards, 36 inches; 1¼ yards, 54 inches.

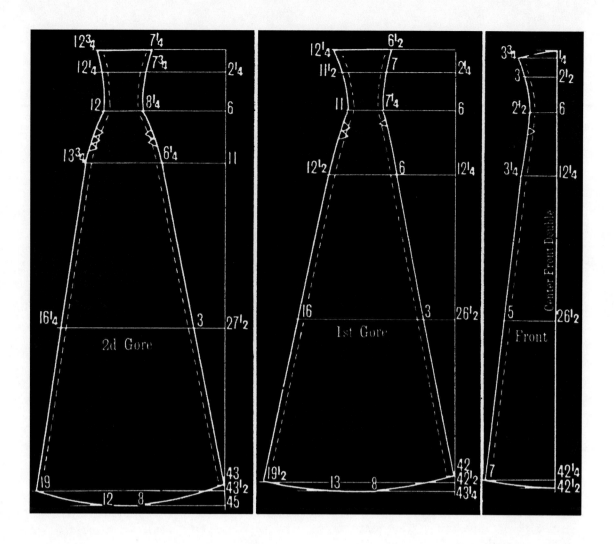

PRINCESS SKIRT.

The diagrams on this page and the preceding page are for a princess skirt, never completely out of vogue, and now apparently "in" for an extended stay. The lines are graceful, and the garment is simply made. It is lined from top down to hips only. The waist part is to be boned. The top may be embellished by scallops or other shaping to suit any fancy, and trimming other than shown in the illustration may be effectively employed. This pattern may be easily used in the reproduction of most of the princess designs seen in the current fashion journals.

Draft by Compound Scale or by general instructions.

Material required for medium size, 10 yards, 22 inches wide; 7 yards, 36 inches; 4¾ yards, 54 inches.

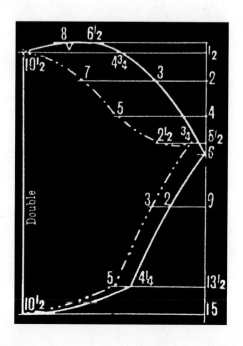

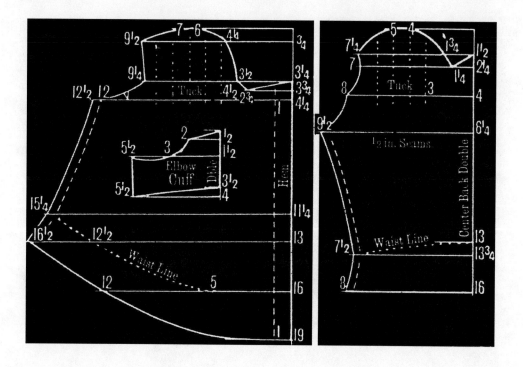

LADIES' COSTUME.

The diagrams on this page and the page following are for a handsome costume for ladies, shown in the illustration with skirt made of plaid worsted suiting of brown and blue, gored, with tunic effect, and trimming of plain blue with stitched bands. The waist is of blue silk. The patterns may be as effectively used, however, for widely different materials.

The body of the waist is tucked in two groups on both back and front, in the shaping of the pretty yoke. These tucks are shown in the diagram. The measurement of the first of these tucks is given in the diagrams. The tucks are 1 space apart. Fold on lines and stitch ¼ space deep. See Explanation of illustrations for sleeve.

Draft waist and sleeve by Compound Scale.

Material required for medium size, waist and sleeve, 4 yards, 22 inches wide; 3 yards, 36 inches; 2 yards, 44 inches.

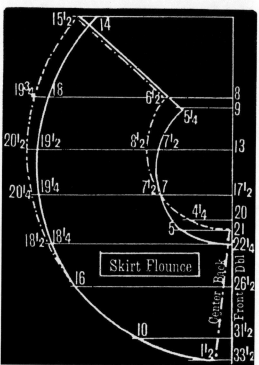

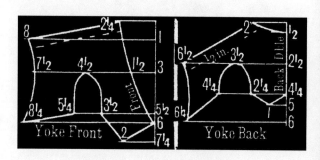

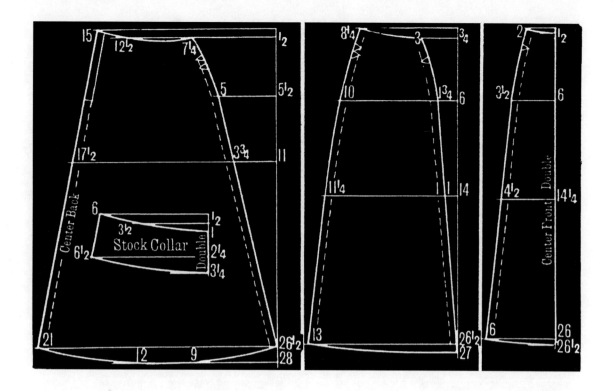

DRAPED SKIRT

The diagrams on this page, with that for skirt flounce on the preceding page, are for a handsome draped skirt. This pattern was originally designed for the ladies' costume described on the preceding page and effectiveely shown in the illustration; but it may be used for other purposes as well, and will be found to be a very useful design. The skirt is of five gores, with a flounce   This part of the pattern may be used for a five-gored skirt to be worn without drapery   The drapery is of tunic effect, growing in favor the present season.

The back and front patterns for the drapery are both in one diagram, as they are in the diagram for flounce. Cut on broken lines in each for the back section of patterns, and on the plain lines for the front sections. Pin the two sections of each together, and cut material on a double fold for the front. Let the piecing seams come where they may. If a hem is wanted on bottom of drapery, allow additional material accordingly.

Draft by general instructions, by bust measure.

Material required for medium size, for drapery and flounce, 8 yards, 22 inches wide; 5½ yards, 36 inches; 4½ yards, 44 inches; for five gores, 4½ yards, 22 inches; 2¾ yards, 36 inches; 2 yards, 44 inches.

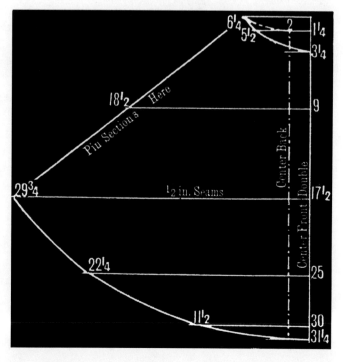

29

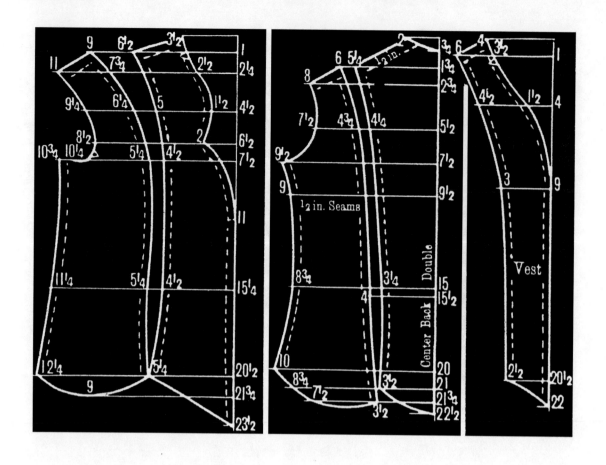

TWO-PIECE COSTUME.

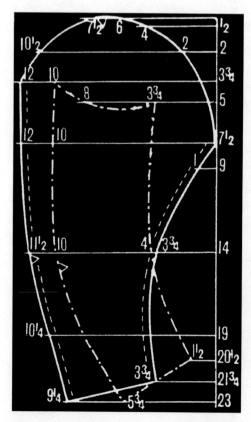

A practical design for a pretty two-piece costume is provided for in the diagrams on this page and the page following. At the present time of extra-elaborate garments this simple yet effective suit will surely be appreciated. The shapely jacket has a vest front of different material, and is trimmed with braid. Stitched straps of the same material as the garment may be used instead of the braid. Other sleeves may be used if desired.

The coat and sleeve are to be drafted by the Compound Scale or by general instructions. The various parts of the coat are joined in the diagrams to save time and labor in the drafting.

This coat may be lengthened with little or no trouble, producing a most effective garment as a long coat.

Material required for the coat, 4½ yards, 22 inches wide; 2¾ yards, 36 inches; 1¾ yards, 50 inches. The vest, if made of other material, will require ¾ yard.

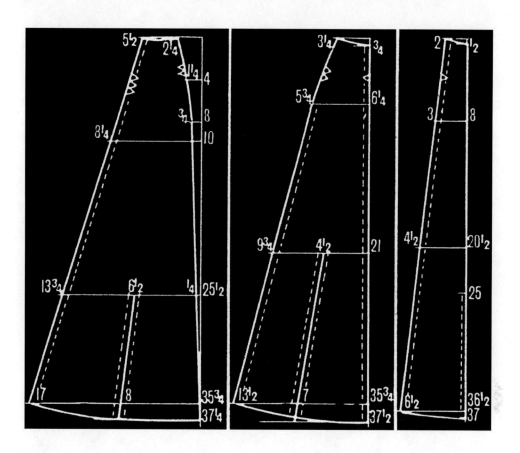

SEVEN-CORED SKIRT.

The diagrams on this page are for a seven-gored skirt, with habit back. It was designed for the pretty two-piece costume on the preceding page, but will be a most useful pattern for other purposes. By adding 3 spaces to the center back at waist, slanting to the bottom, an inverted box pleat may be produced in place of the habit back. Each gore is slashed to a length shown in the diagrams, and in these slashes are insets forming inverted box pleats to provide a fulness, or flare, at the bottom so much in vogue at this time. The diagrams show the length of each inset, and they are to be of 10 spaces in width.

The pattern may be used for a plain seven-gored skirt without the slashes and insets.

Material required for medium size, 8 yards, 22 inches wide; 5½ yards, 36 inches; 4 yards, 50 inches.

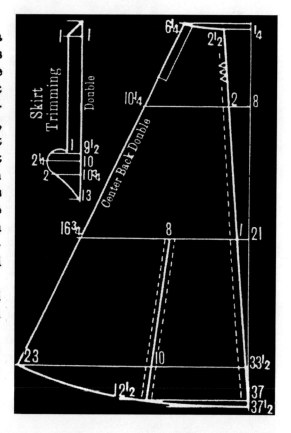

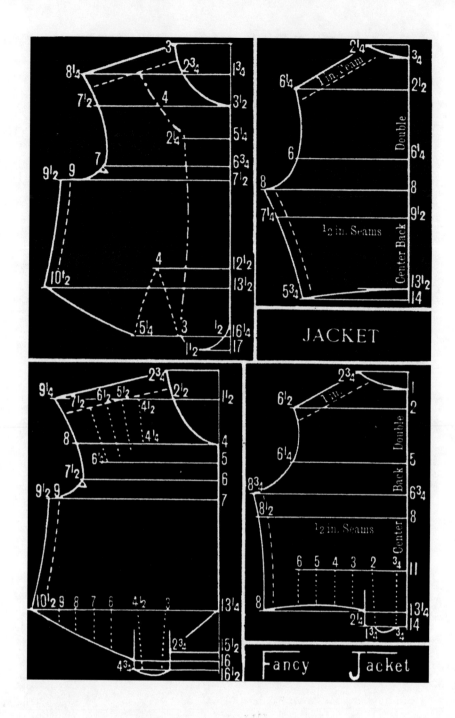

JACKET

Fancy Jacket

LADIES' COSTUME.

On this page and the two following pages are diagrams for a simple but "smart" costume for ladies. The patterns may also be very effectively used for misses. It has a pretty jacket of the Eton variety, with vest front. The skirt is one of the best of the new circular design, close around the hips, with a slight fulness at center back, and a flare at bottom. The diagrams for skirt are made for two lengths. The trimming for skirt and jacket are of braid. The jacket is finished with stitched bands of the same material, for which diagrams are given on the second page following this.

The above diagrams are for both a plain and a fancy jacket. The plain pattern is to be used for the lining of the fancy garment. A broken line on diagram for front of this plain pattern is for the vest front. The fancy jacket has a tab on each side of back and front. These tabs are slashed up to permit the stitched trimming to pass under. The dotted lines in the diagrams are for pin-tucks and for box-pleat folds for the tabs.

Draft jacket and sleeve by Compound Scale or general instructions.

Material required for medium size jacket, 3½ yards, 22 inches wide; 2½ yards, 36 inches; 1¾ yards, 50 inches.

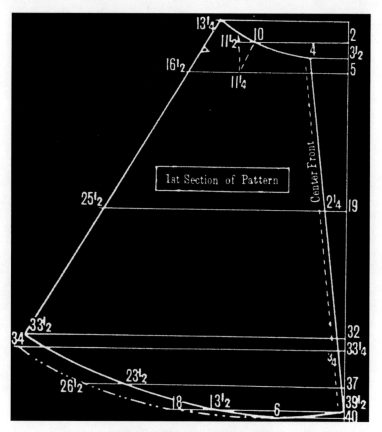

CIRCULAR SKIRT.

These diagrams are for circular skirts of the latest design, further described on the preceding page. The two sections of pattern are to be pinned together before cutting material, letting the piecing come wherever it may. For skirt with seam down front, lay on pattern just as it is placed in the diagram, the front biased. To cut without the center seam, fold under pattern at front seam line and lay on fold of the material. Material required for medium size, 6 yards, 22 inches wide; 4¾ yards, 36 inches; 4 yards, 50 inches.

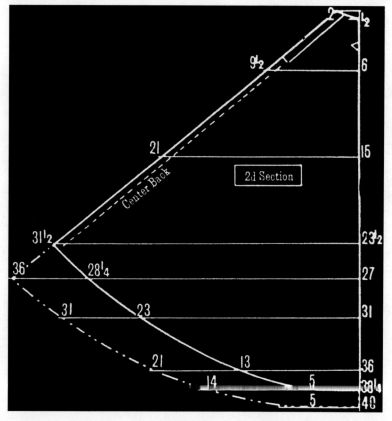

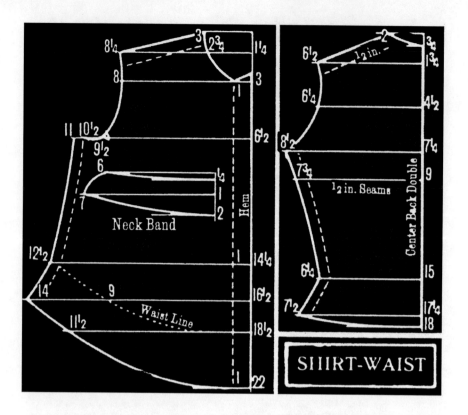

PLAIN SHIRT WAIST.

The above diagram is for a plain shirt waist for ladies or misses. It would seem unnecessary to continue to refer to the usefulness of a plain pattern, being adapted to so many uses. Little skill is required to tuck or pleat material according to fancy before cutting; but, having some skill, the maker may copy in this way from any of the fashion journals innumerable designs. Whenever, in the Explanation of Illustrations in this book, the direction is given to tuck or pleat goods before cutting, it *necessarily* follows that the pattern then used must be a *plain* pattern.

Draft by Compound Scale or by general instructions.

The sleeve and trimming in the diagrams at foot of page are for the ladies' costume described on the two preceding pages.

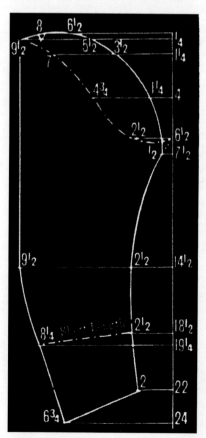

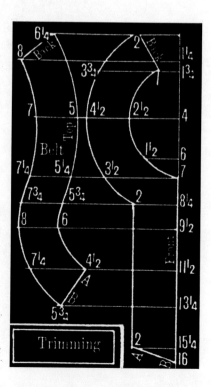

34

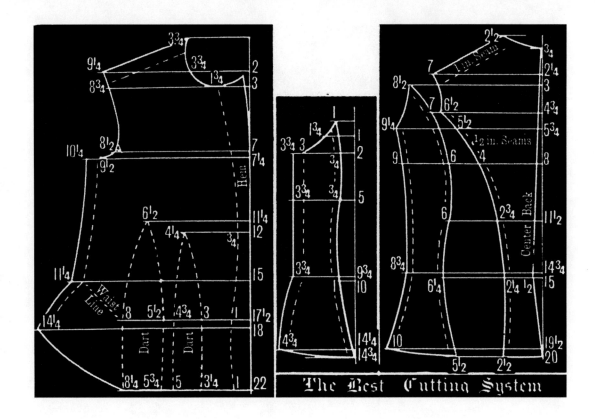

LADIES' FITTED BASQUE.

The diagrams on this page are for a new basque, the pattern for which is alone worth much more than the price of the book. Those who talk about this, that, and the other "chart" or "model" will find in this one pattern all that can be had in any of the so-called "systems" of cutting. In view of present tenden-cies of fashion, this pattern promises to become more and more useful. The length is given so as to extend over the hips when desired. The waist-line for the back is at 15; for the side-back, at 14¾; for the under-arm at 10, running up to 3¾ on line 9¾; on front at line 17½ in front, running up from second dart to 11¼ on line 15. Dart lines may be changed, if needed, without interfering with any other part of the garment.

Draft either by general instructions or by Com-pound Scale, for which instructions are given in front part of this book.

Amount of material for medium size, with sleeve, 3 yards, 22 inches wide; 2 yards, 36 inches; 1½ yards, 50 inches.

The adjoining pattern is for plain sleeve, which may be used for linings or a plain dress sleeve.

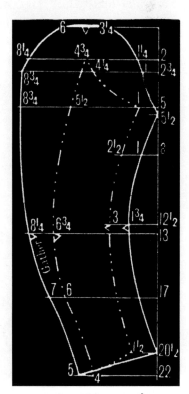

DRESS SLEEVE.

35

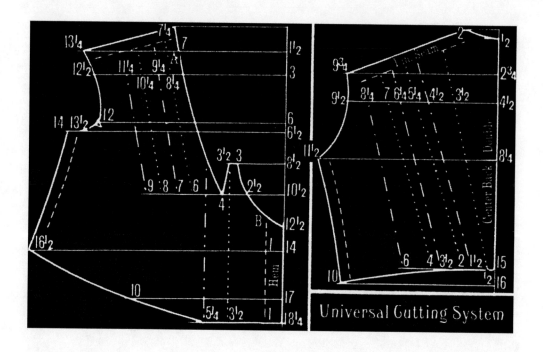

Universal Cutting System

LADIES' COSTUME.

A most effective gown for ladies, as shown in the illustration, may be developed by the aid of the diagrams given on this page and the two pages following. It has a bodice with a deep girdle, and is tucked over the shoulder both front and back. It has a vest front with a pretty shoulder collar and shapely front trimming. This trimming forms part of the waist front, and may be of the same material, or varied to suit the taste of the maker. The skirt has a box-pleated front, and has two circular portions with a side-pleated flounce. The upper circular portion is applied over the other, and may be omitted if preferred. The circular portions may be made plain or scalloped. The diagrams are made plain, with a detail for scallops enclosed. In laying the pleats, fold on the dotted lines and lay over to the broken lines. Letters and notches show where parts of pattern are to be joined.

Draft waist and sleeve by Compound Scale, and skirt by general instructions. Change length of skirt at bottom of front section and the flounce.

See following page for further directions.

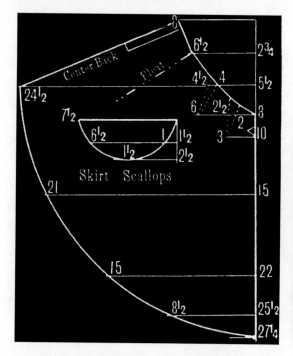

Skirt Scallops

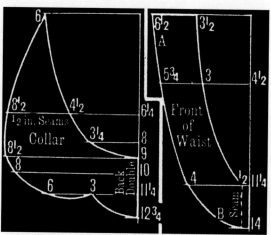

36

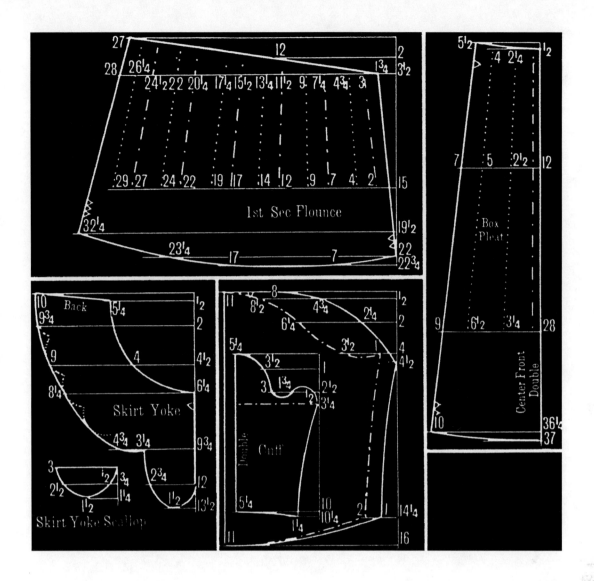

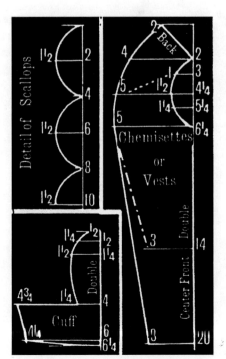

The diagrams above are for the skirt front and first section of flounce for the ladies' costume described on the preceding page; also for skirt yoke and sleeve. The diagrams are given with such details as to require no further directions here.

Material required for medium size, waist, 3½ yards, 27 inches wide; 3 yards, 36 inches; 2 yards, 50 inches.

VEST AND CUFF

The adjoining diagrams are for a vest and a cuff. That for vest is given in two shapes. The pattern will be found very useful and is referred to in various places in the Explanations of Illustrations.

The diagram for a cuff is for a pretty though an odd shape, designed for the sleeve shown in the illustration, but the pattern will be found useful for other sleeves.

37

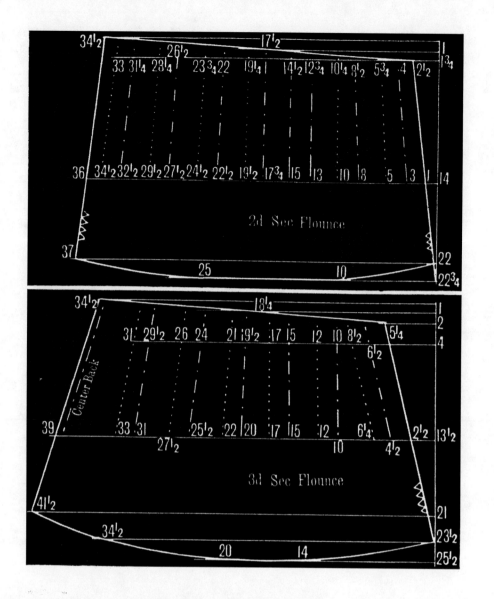

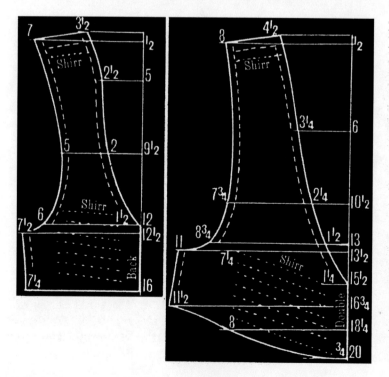

The diagrams above are for the second and third sections of the skirt for ladies' costume described on the two preceding pages.

Material for medium size, 10 yards, 27 inches wide; 8 yards, 36 inches; 6 yards, 50 inches.

GIRDLE.

The adjoining diagram is for a girdle with suspenders—a useful pattern at present. It is to be shirred as indicated by the dotted lines.

Material required, 1¾ yards, 24 inches wide; 1¼ yards, 44 inches.

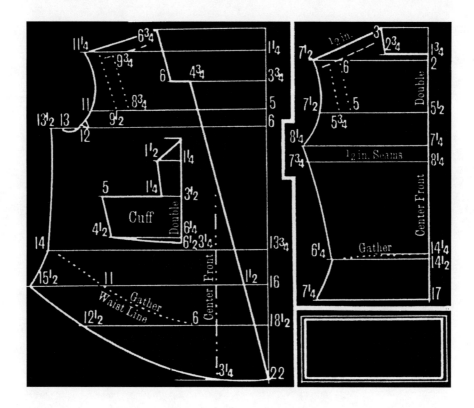

SURPLICE WAIST.

The diagrams above are for the body part of a surplice waist of effective design. It is worn over a tucked chemisette, which may be of the same material or of contrasting material. This is a very simple pattern, easily made. The illustration shows a narrow tuck over the shoulder, back and front. It is ornamented with buttons. The diagram for sleeve shown in the principal illustration of this waist will be found on another page. (See Explanation of Illustrations.) The diagram for cuff is given above. For the tuck at shoulder, fold between the dotted lines in diagram and stitch on the lines.

Draft by Compound Scale or general instructions.

Material required for medium size, 4 yards, 22 inches wide; 2½ yards, 36 inches; 1¾ yards, 50 inches.

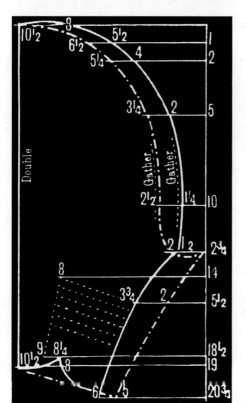

FANCY SLEEVE.

An extremely stylish elbow sleeve is the design for which the adjoining diagram was made, but by using a pattern for a plain sleeve for an extension a beautiful full-length sleeve may be developed. Dotted lines are given for a series of pin tucks at lower part of sleeve. The lace trimming shown in the illustration is applied to the lining.

39

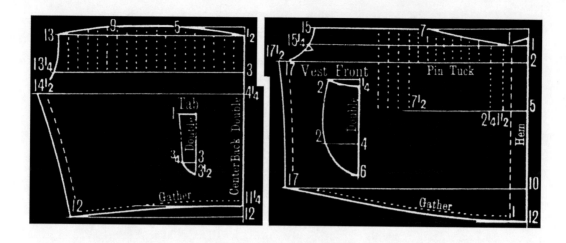

YOKE WAIST.

A yoke waist for either ladies or misses is provided for in the diagrams on this page. As shown in the illustration there is a prettily shaped yoke with a tucked shield in front. Diagrams for the yoke will be seen below. The fulness of the body of the waist is disposed of in a series of pin tucks ¾ space apart. The groups of four at center front and on each side are covered by a pointed tab, for which a diagram is given above. The "Gigot" sleeve is trimmed at wrist by a pin-tucked ornament, for which a diagram is given. Notches show where this is to be attached.

Broken lines of the front for yoke show where it may be cut for a plain yoke; but this pretty shape may be utilized in connection with other patterns for waists. The body of waist may be gathered in instead of tucked, or the yoke may be used over body part tucked otherwise and trimmed to suit any wish.

Draft by Compound Scale or general instructions.

Material required for medium size, 4 yards, 22 inches wide; 2½ yards, 36 inches; 1¾ yards, 50 inches.

The diagram for sleeve may be used for a plain leg-o'-mutton pattern by cutting on the dotted line at bottom.

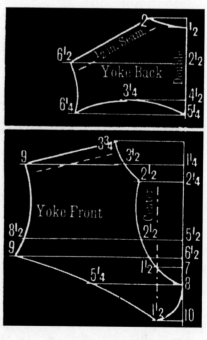

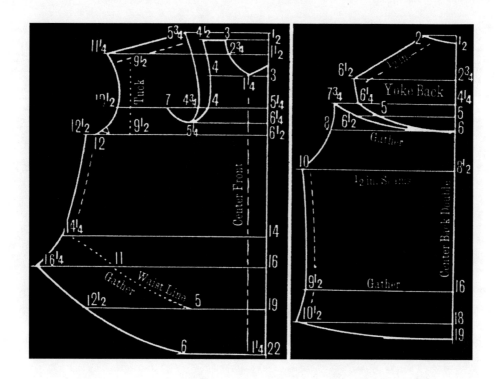

FANCY WAIST.

A very pretty design for a fancy waist may be developed from the diagrams given above, with a sleeve and cuff given elsewhere in this book. (See Explanation of Illustrations.) The waist has a tuck of ½ space at the arm reaching to the shoulder seam. The front is slashed as shown in the diagram, the upper part being brought down over the gathered lower part, forming a pretty ornament. The front closing is concealed by an applied pleat of 2 spaces in width when completed. It has a yoke back.

Draft by Compound Scale or general instructions.

Material required for medium size, 3¾ yards, 22 inches wide; 3 yards, 36 inches; 2 yards, 50 inches.

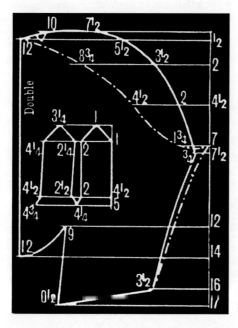

FANCY SLEEVE.

The diagrams for a fancy sleeve, given here, are for an exceptionally pretty design. A special diagram is given for the close lower part of the sleeve with tabs, to overlap the upper part. A pattern for a plain sleeve may be used for lining.

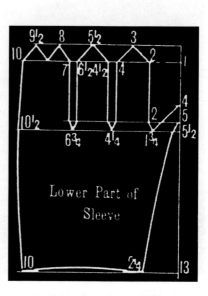

41

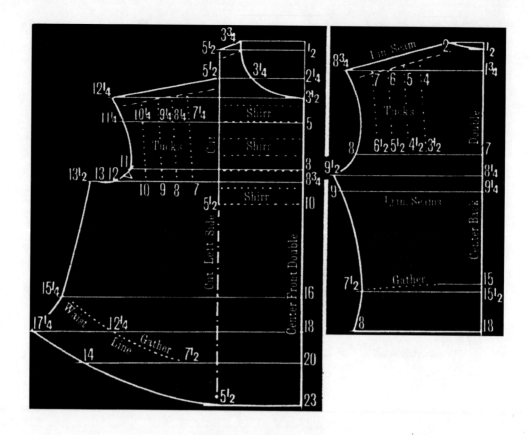

FANCY WAIST.

The fancy waist provided for by the diagrams on this page is to be made with tucks over the shoulders and a shirred front. The sleeve is of the leg-o'-mutton shape, with a pretty strap to cover the few gathers at elbow. The pattern may be used to develop a garment even more elaborately ornamented, and the garment may be made of plain material as well as of that shown in the illustration. The waist is closed on

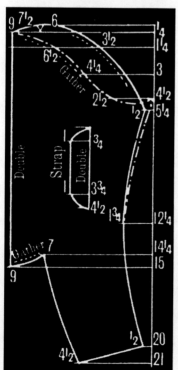

the left side. Both sides for front are to be cut open on the plain line, and the left side only is to be cut on the broken line of the diagram, as directed there. The tucks on both front and back are to be folded and stitched ¼ space deep. It is shirred into the neck, and other lines of shirring are 1 space apart. Pin tucks are made and shirred to follow the neck instead of straight as given in the diagram. The diagram for sleeve does not allow for the four small tucks at wrist. For these tucks allow 2 spaces at lower part of sleeve, and take up ½ space in each tuck, stitching ¼ space deep, for sleeve shown in the illustration.

Material required for medium size, 4 yards, 22 inches wide; 3 yards, 36 inches; 2 yards, 50 inches.

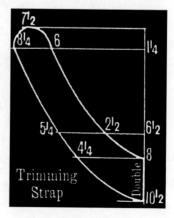

42

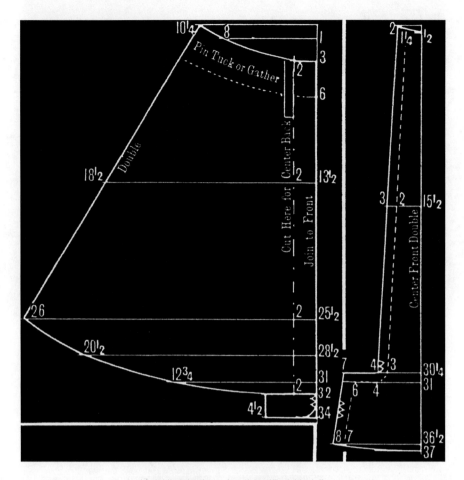

LADIES' COSTUME.

A very smart and serviceable costume for ladies is provided for by the diagrams for skirt on this page and those for the waist given on another page in this book. The waist is described in connection with the diagrams given, for which see Explanation of Illustrations. The skirt has a front panel, with circular sides, with a pretty flounce. The panel is shaped at bottom most effectively. Any desired material from prints to silks may be used to develop this gown.

For ease of drafting, the diagram is given for cutting the circular section in two pieces, to be pinned together before cutting the material. Draft according to the diagram, then cut double, making two patterns. Cut off one of these at the broken line, pin the two together where the word "double" appears, and then cut the material. The same is done in cutting the flounce, below.

Draft skirt by general instructions—not by Compound Scale.

Material required for medium size, 7 yards, 27 inches wide; 5 yards, 36 inches; 4¼ yards, 50 inches.

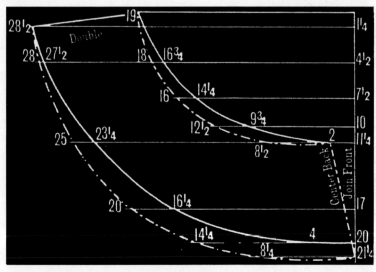

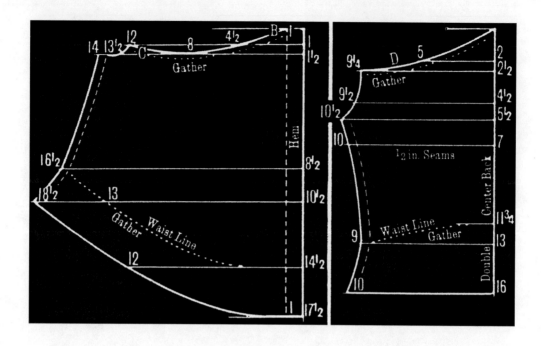

YOKE WAIST.

The diagrams on this page are for an exceedingly pretty yoke waist for ladies or misses. The yoke is in one piece. The illustration shows the yoke to be ornamented by faggot-stitching. This yoke may be of plain material the same as body of waist, or of any other material suitable to go with the body part. It may be of all-over lace. In fact, the pattern is such that the garment may be developed in a dozen different ways most effectively. As shown in the illustration, the yoke is attached to the body part under bands of embroidery, and the sleeves are ornamented with the same material. Letters on the diagrams for yoke and body part indicate where the parts are to be joined.

The diagram for sleeve, given below, is specially designed for the short cuff given in the diagram, and the length is regulated for that special cuff. If a longer cuff is desired the length of the sleeve should be shortened accordingly.

Draft waist and sleeve by Compound Scale or by general instructions, as desired.

Amount of material for medium size, 3½ yards, 22 inches wide; 3 yards, 36 inches; 2 yards, 44 inches.

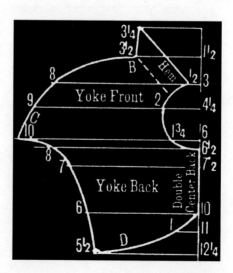

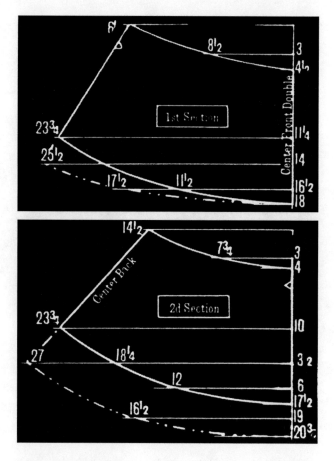

PETTICOAT, OR SLIP SKIRT.

The diagrams on this page are for a petticoat, or slip skirt, with flounces. This is a model much in demand now. The flounces are not very full, being intended for the application of additional fulness by the use of ruffles on the flounce. It may be made as full or elaborate as desired, to suit the garment with which it is to be worn. The circular portion is in one piece, while the diagrams for flounces are made in two parts for convenience of drafting. Pin together the two parts of pattern for flounces before cutting. The flounce patterns are given in two lengths.

Draft by general instructions—not by Compound Scale.

Material required for medium size, single flounce, sweep length, 5 yards, 27 inches wide; 3¾ yards, 36 inches.

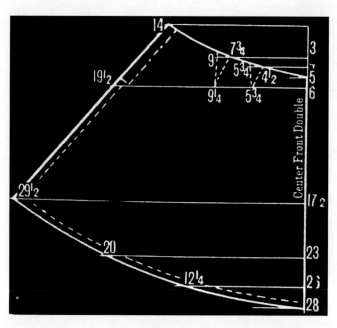

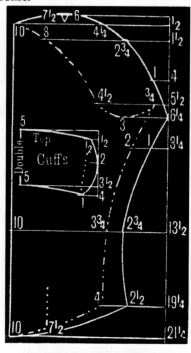

SHIRT WAIST SLEEVE.

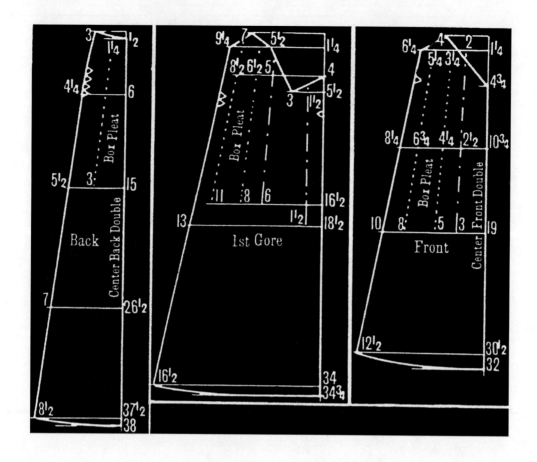

YOKE SKIRT.

The diagrams on this page and the page following are for a handsome yoke skirt with box pleats. As shown in the illustration, it is of round length. The box pleats when folded form points which are extended over the yoke, as shown in the illustration. A dotted line in the diagram which is marked "hem" is for the seam where the skirt is attached to the yoke. In making the seams, begin at bottom and seam upwards. Fold pleats on the dotted lines and lay over each way to the broken lines, forming box pleats. The placket is made under the box pleat in center back.

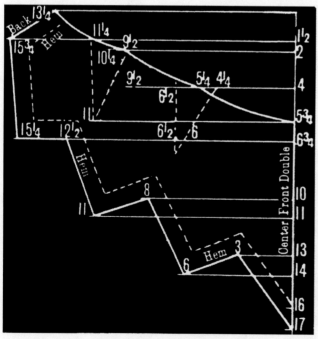

Fold under ½ inch on upper part of skirt portion and attach to yoke by stitching through and through, on the dotted line 1 space from bottom.

The points of the box pleat extend upwards over the yoke as shown in the illustration, and are to be stitched to a depth of 9 inches to hold them in position.

See next page for further directions.

SKIRT YOKE.

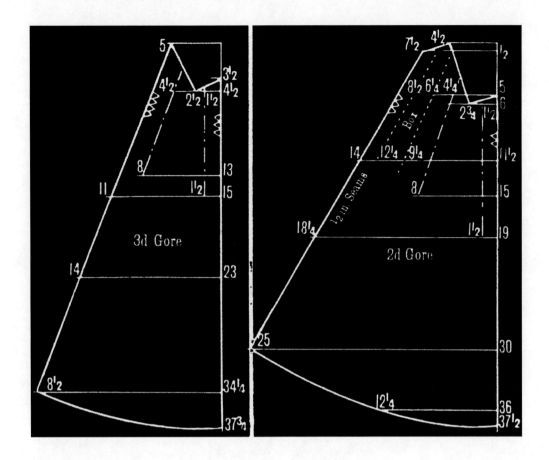

The diagrams above are for the eight-gored skirt described on the preceding page. As represented in the illustration this skirt has three tucks, each 1 space wide when finished. There is also a hem 3 spaces wide at bottom. The tucks and hem are not provided for in the diagrams. If these tucks and hem are wanted additional material will have to be allowed, which will be 9 spaces on each gore.

Amount of material for medium size, 9½ yards, 27 inches wide; 7 yards, 36 inches; 5 yards, 50 inches.

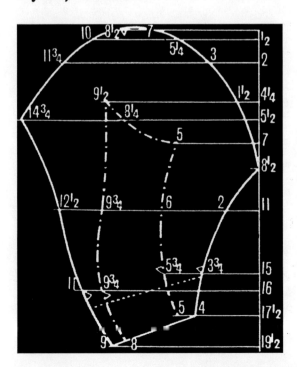

SHORT SLEEVE.

The adjoining diagram is for short sleeves. It is a two-seam sleeve, and may be made with or without a lining. It may be finished at bottom with an elbow cuff, with frills of lace, or finished in any way desired to make a sleeve of much elegance.

Cut pattern at dotted line, allowing for a seam, for an elbow-length.

Material required, 1½ yards, 22 inches wide; ¾ yards, 44 inches.

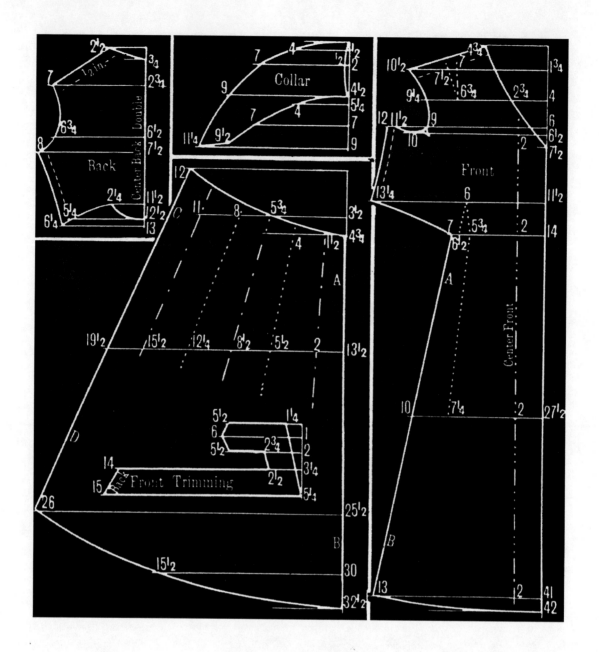

EMPIRE COAT.

The diagrams on this page and the page following are for a most effective coat, double-breasted, with handsome sleeves. As shown in the illustration, the collar and cuffs are of fur, but may be made of the same material as the body of the garment, or other suitable material. The trimming shown in the illustration is of wide silk braid; but the garment may be trimmed with any other material. The trimming may be varied in form, or made with merely rows of stitching. The illustration is for one suggestion.

Diagrams for the bands of trimming will be found within the other diagrams. Skilled makers may cut the trimmings without resorting to the careful drafting of such parts.

If the pleats are not wanted the pleats may be folded in the pattern, producing a good pattern for a plain, semi-fitting coat. The lining for the waist part is to be cut by the patterns for the outside.

In putting together, care should be observed as to the letters which show how the parts of the skirt of garment are to be joined.

The pattern may be drafted by Compound Scale, but the length at bottom should be regulated by tape line measurement, as the coat is to be made longer or shorter, according to fancy.

Draft by Compound Scale or by general instructions.

Amount of material for medium size, 8½ yards, 27 inches wide; 5 yards, 44 inches; 4 yards, 54 inches.

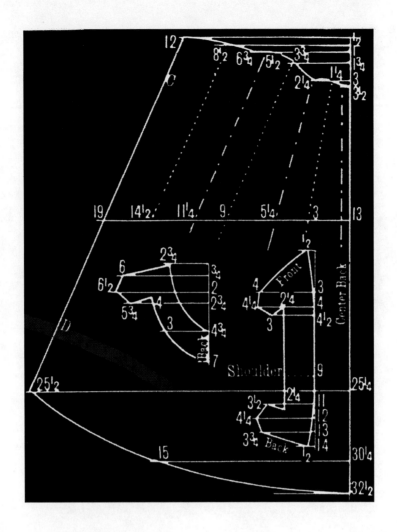

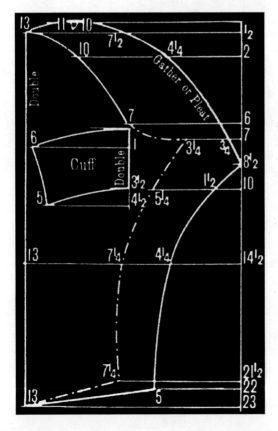

The diagrams on this page are for the Empire Coat described on the preceding page.

In making the coat, join together the two sections of the skirt and then lay the pleats in them before joining to the front section. For the pleats fold on the dotted lines and lay backward to the broken lines and stitch ½ space from the edge to a depth of 8 or 10 inches.

The three tucks in the sleeve, as shown in the illustration, are to be laid 2 spaces apart and stitch ¾ space deep. The third pleat is to be laid at 13 on line 23 in the diagram. Instead of the pleats the goods may be gathered in to the top of the cuff.

Draft sleeve by Compound Scale or general instructions.

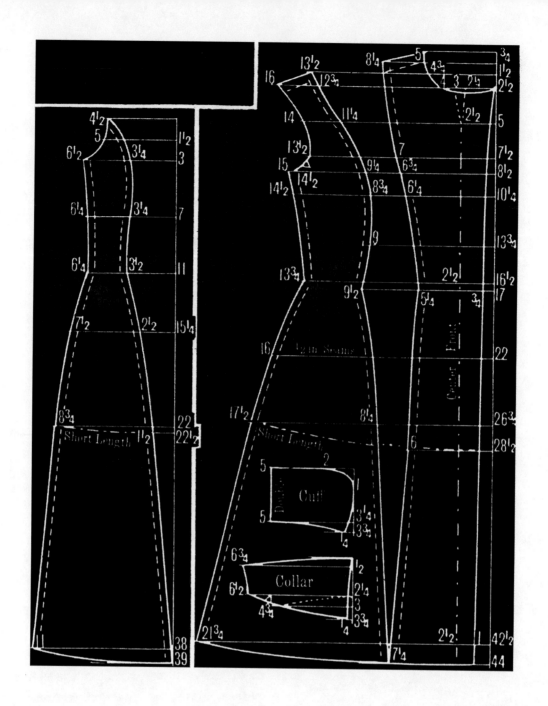

LADIES' COAT

The diagrams on this page and the page following are for a close-fitted coat for ladies or misses. It has seams over the shoulders reaching to bottom of the garment in both front and back. The back, below the waist-line, is open in center, with a lap, and has inverted pleats at the side-back seams. The front laps well, fastening with flys underneath. Dotted lines on the diagram for sleeve, on following page, show where small pleats, folding each way from the notch, to form a box pleat at top of shoulder. The style of this garment may be varied by different collars or cuffs, shown in the different illustrations given. Broken lines in the diagrams show where the pattern may be shortened for a pretty, short coat.

Draft by Compound Scale or general instructions.

Material required for medium size, 7½ yards, 27 inches wide; 4¼ yards, 44 inches; 3½ yards, 50 inches.

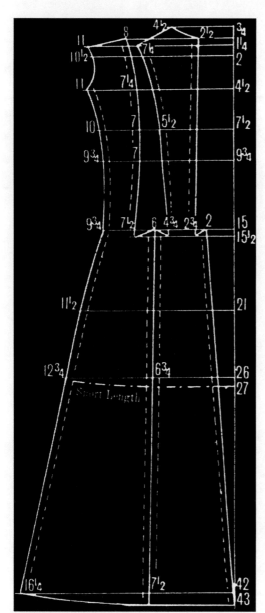

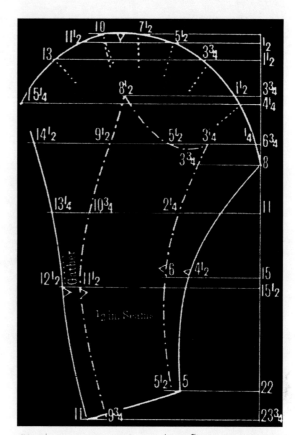

The diagrams at the head of this page are for the ladies' coat described on the preceding page, and need no further explanation.

A diagram for a plain short sleeve, the pattern for which may be used for a lining for fancy short sleeves, is given below.

The pattern for a full vest, to be gathered or shirred into the neck, is given below.

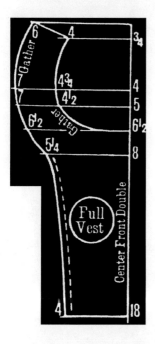

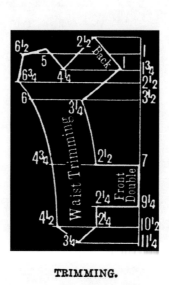

TRIMMING.

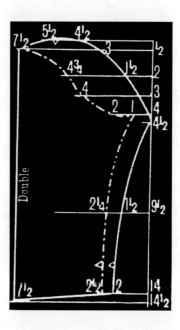

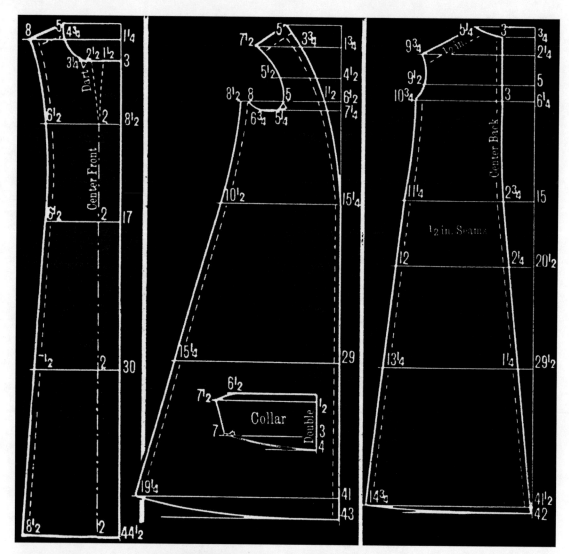

LADIES' ULSTER COAT.

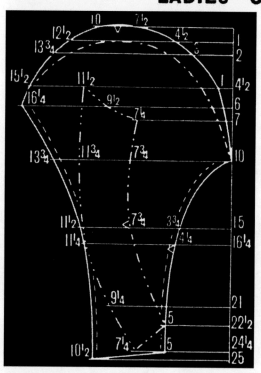

LEG-O'-MUTTON SLEEVE FOR DRESS.

These diagrams are for an ulster coat, and the pattern may be used for a rain coat or any sort of a general utility coat, being plain, simple, and easily made. It has a seam over the shoulder reaching to the bottom of garment. The garment may be embellished with trimming if desired, and thus be made suitable for expensive material and elaborate workmanship. Other collars may be used instead of that for which a diagram is given here. See Explanation of Illustrations for sleeve.

Draft by Compound Scale or general instructions.

Material required for medium size, 7½ yards, 27 inches wide; 4¼ yards, 44 inches; 3¾ yards, 54 inches.

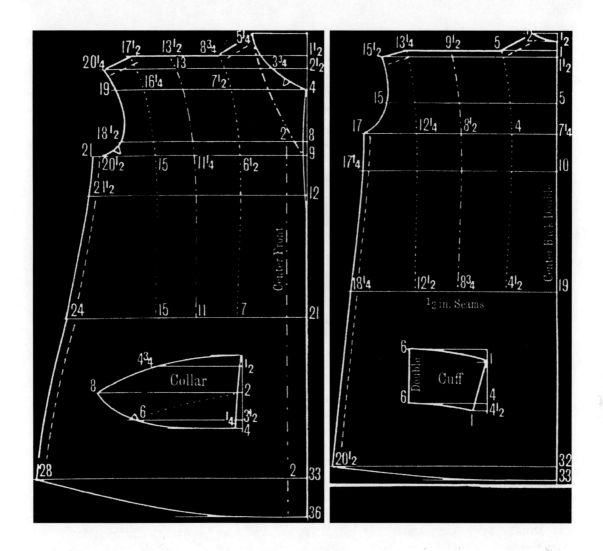

BOX COAT.

The diagrams above are for a box coat with inverted pleats in front and back. A plain coat may be made from this pattern by folding the pleats in the pattern before cutting the material. This pattern is a most excellent design, from which the garment may be easily developed. Fold the pleats on the dotted lines and lay over to meet at the broken line. Stitch through ¼ space from the edge. For sleeve see Explanation of Illustrations.

Draft by Compound Scale or general instructions.

Material required for miss of fourteen, 5½ yards, 27 inches wide; 4 yards, 40 inches; 3½ yards, 50 inches.

WIDE BELT.

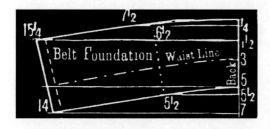

The diagram for belt foundation adjoining is an important feature of the prevailing modes. It is cut from a bias piece of crinoline. A broken line lengthwise of diagram shows where tapes are to be stitched on to the width of 1 inch as a stay. Other material may be used in place of tape. The front ends are to be finished with firm material for eyelets or hooks and eyes. Featherbone or whalebone is to be used in front, back, and on each side to hold in the broad tape. Drape this for a crush belt with silk or other material.

53

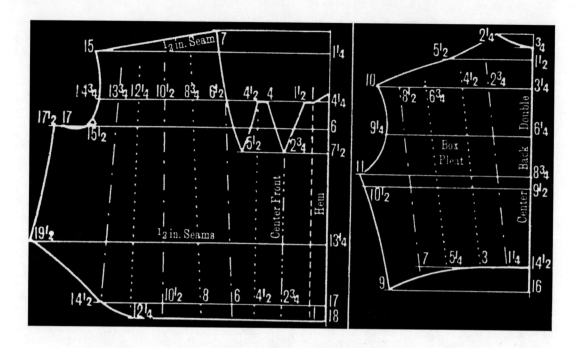

MISSES' SUIT.

The diagrams on this page and the following page are for a very pretty suit for misses, which may as well be used for ladies by lengthening the skirt. The waist is double-breasted. For left side fold under pattern at center front. The backward-turned pleats are to be folded on dotted lines and laid back to broken lines, and then pressed or stitched. See Explanation of Illustrations for collar and cuff.

The skirt is of eleven gores, side pleated, the pleats being either stitched or merely pressed. For pleats fold on dotted lines and lay back to broken lines. A pleat is made to cover each of the seams.

Draft waist, skirt, and sleeve by Compound Scale or by general instructions.

Material required for miss of sixteen years, waist, 3¾ yards, 27 inches wide; 3 yards, 36 inches; 2 yards, 54 inches. Skirt, without piecing, 11½ yards, 27 inches wide; 8 yards, 36 inches; 5½ yards, 54 inches.

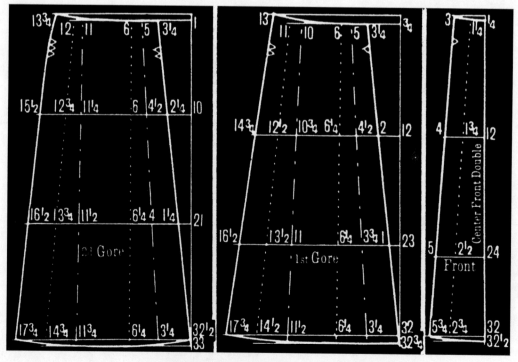

ELEVEN-GORED SKIRT.

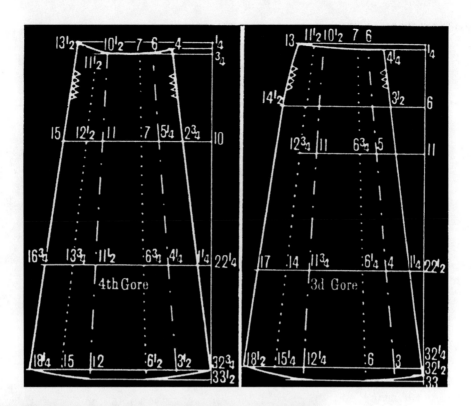

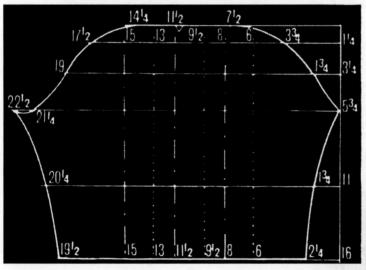

The diagrams on this page are for the misses' costume described on the preceding page. The diagram for sleeve, given above, is for a high cuff. A diagram for cuff may be found on another page—see Explanation of Illustrations.

This sleeve may be either pleated or gathered.

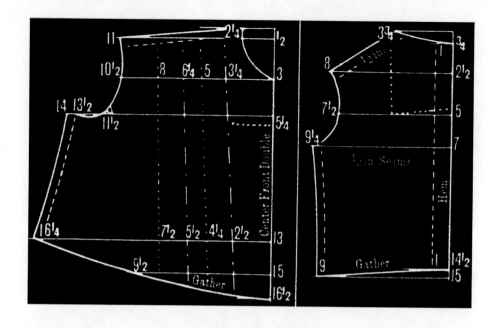

GIRLS' DRESS.

A very useful pattern for a dress for girls, and for misses, may be made from the diagrams on this page and the page following. As shown in the illustration, the skirt is of the short length for girls or young misses, but may readily be lengthened to suit any purpose. The diagrams provide for a skirt somewhat longer than shown in the illustration. The pretty waist has bretelles over the shoulders, with a center piece in both front and back. The trimming in front is black buttons and silk cord. If a chemisette is used with the garment, cut out the waist in front and back as provided by the dotted lines in diagrams. The waist is fastened in the back underneath the panel piece. The tucks in waist are folded on the dotted lines and laid back to broken lines, and stitched to yoke depth. A diagram below marked "trimming" is for both back and front panels, the dotted line being for the back panel.

The waist and sleeve may both be drafted by the Compound Scale, as well as by general instructions.

Amount of material for waist and sleeve, 3½ yards, 22 inches wide; 2¼ yards, 36 inches; 1¾ yards, 50 inches.

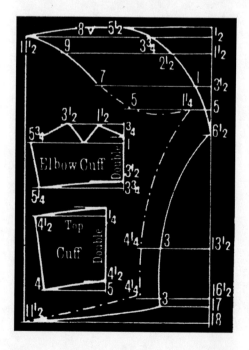

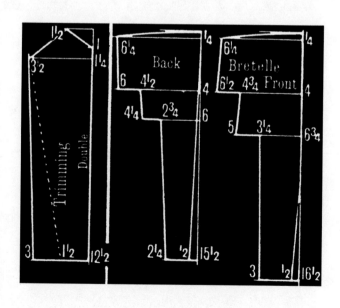

56

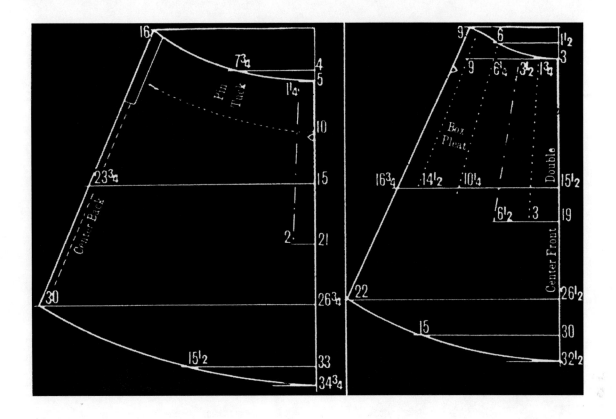

MISSES' CIRCULAR SKIRT.

The circular skirt for which the above diagrams provide was designed especially for the dress for girls described on the preceding page. It will prove a very good pattern for a skirt to be worn with other waists as well. It has three box pleats, one in center front and one on each side. The fulness in sides and back may be gathered or pin tucked, as desired. Fold on the dotted lines for pleats and lay over each way to the broken lines.

Draft by Compound Scale or by general instructions. Pin together the two sections of pattern before cutting material.

Material required for girl of twelve years, 4 yards, 22 inches wide; 3 yards, 36 inches; 2¼ yards, 50 inches.

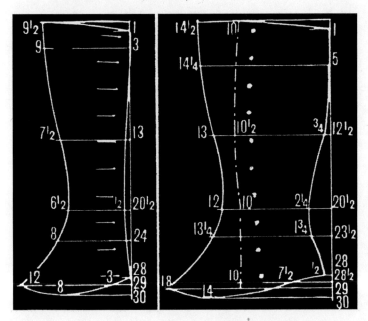

LEGGINGS.

The adjoining diagrams are for leggings, or over-gaiters. The larger diagram is for the inside part and the smaller for the front of the outside. For the back of the outside cut on the broken line of the larger diagram. On this part the buttons are attached. For gaiters cut off at line 12½. Draft by scale corresponding with the largest part of the calf of the leg.

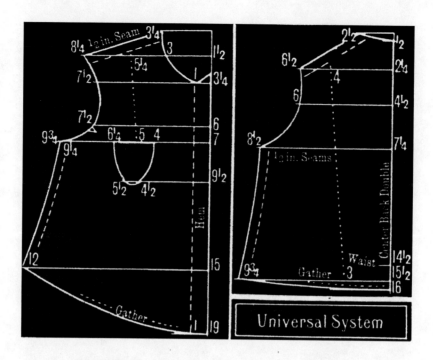

GIRLS' SHIRT-WAIST SUIT.

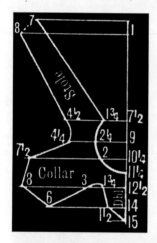

On this page are the diagrams for a most attractive shirt-waist suit for girls and for misses. The waist has an applied shoulder piece, or collar, with stole front. In the diagram for this trimming the stole part will be extended so as to reach the waist. Other trimming is to be applied in the form of stitched straps, 1 space wide, over the dotted lines given in the diagrams for back and front. Lines are given for tucks in skirt, in groups of three, the figure for the first of each group being given. See Explanation of Illustrations for sleeve. Draft skirt by general instructions, the waist by Compound Scale.

Material required for girl of thirteen years, 5 yards, 27 inches wide; 4 yards, 36 inches; 3¼ yards, 44 inches.

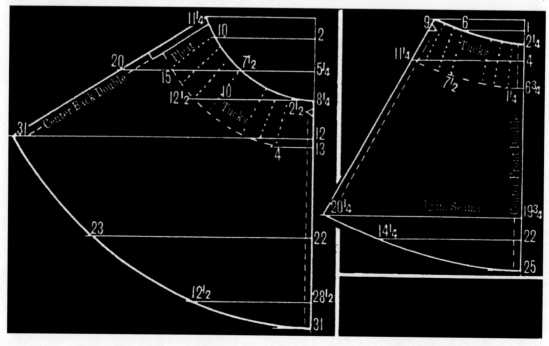

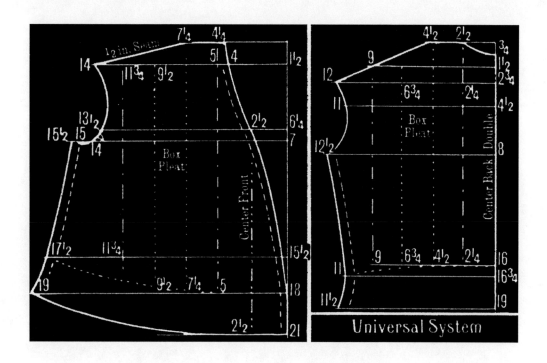

CIRLS' DRESS.

On this page are diagrams for a box-pleated dress for girls. It has a bloused waist with a surplice closing. It is to be worn over a front shield, which may be of tucked cashmere of a harmonizing or a lighter shade. It has a pretty sailor collar and trimmed cuffs. Lines in the diagrams are given for the box pleats for back and front of both waist and skirt. In making these box pleats, fold on the dotted lines of the diagrams and fold to the adjoining broken lines and press. If a side-pleated skirt is wanted, fold on each line and turn backward half way to the next line. The collar and sleeve are given on the following page.

Draft by scale corresponding with bust measure, according to general instructions.

Material required for girl of eight years, 4½ yards, 27 inches wide; 3¼ yards, 36 inches; 2¾ yards, 44 inches.

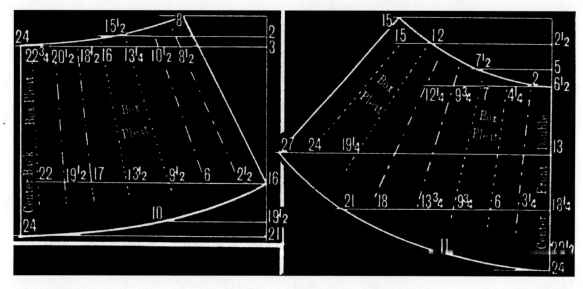

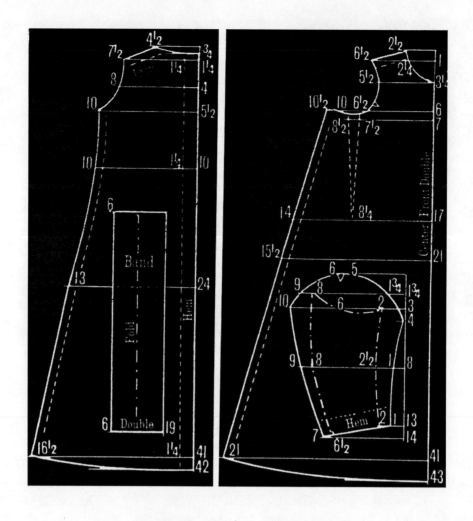

CREEPING APRON.

The diagrams above are for an infants' creeping apron. This very useful pattern has been asked for by numerous patrons. The bottom of the garment is gathered into a band, and, in putting on, this band is adjusted around the body of the child, under the clothing, leaving the feet and limbs free.

Draft by scale corresponding to bust measure, by general instructions.

Amount of material required, 2¼ yards, 27 inches wide; 1¾ yards, 36 inches.

The diagrams for collar and sleeve given below are for the girls' dress described on the preceding page.

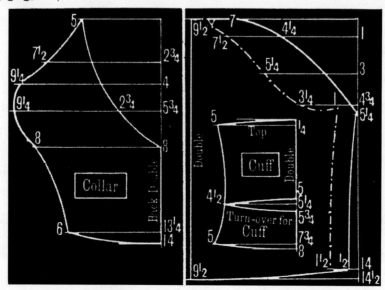

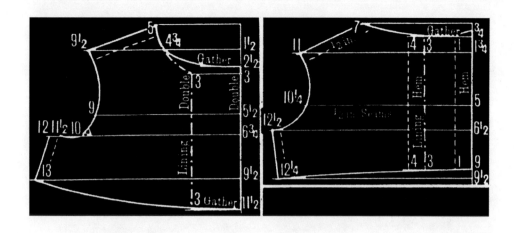

CHILD'S EMPIRE DRESS

A very serviceable pattern for a child's Empire dress is provided for in the diagrams above, with that for sleeve below. Both the outside and the lining for the waist are provided for in the diagrams, broken lines showing where the pattern is to be folded for the lining. A plain waist without lining may be made by using the folded pattern, and the full waist may be made without lining if desired. A line on the diagram for the sleeve shows where it may be cut for a child's puff sleeve, as shown in one illustration. The skirt needs no pattern, it being simply a straight skirt 20 spaces long (hem added) and 40 spaces in width.

Draft waist and sleeve by general instructions, by scale corresponding to bust measure.

Material required for girl of four years, 3½ yards, 27 inches wide; 2¾ yards, 36 inches; 2 yards, 44 inches.

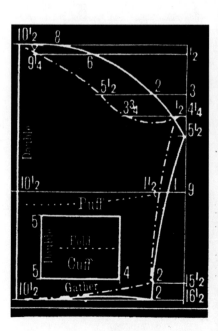

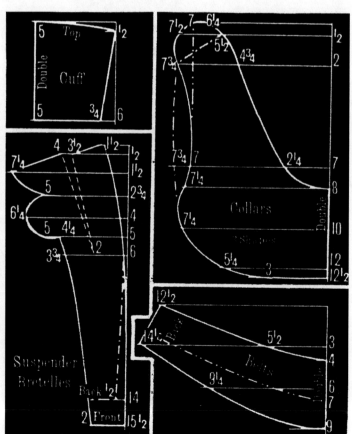

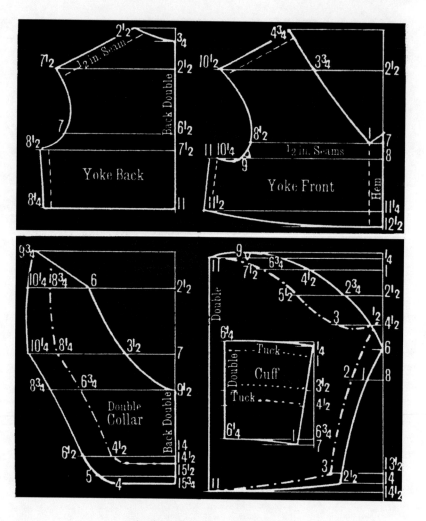

EMPIRE COAT

The diagrams here given are for an Empire coat for either misses or girls. The Empire models are extremely popular at this time, and will continue so indefinitely, a relief from the monotony of the box, semi-fitting and close-fitting models so long in vogue. The illustration shown is for girls only; but the pattern may be used even for ladies by lengthening. This shows the superior advantages of the Universal System, as there is no other system of cutting by which patterns may be adapted to all emergencies.

There is a box pleat both back and front. Fold on dotted lines, and lay over to broken lines and press or stitch. A double collar is shown in the illustration and is provided for in the diagram; but a single collar may be trimmed on the broken line to simulate a double collar. A diagram for half of belt is given. The belt is folded on the dotted lines to form the tab in both back and front. The tucks on cuff are each ½ space wide. The upper tuck is stitched to the sleeve.

Draft by general instructions. Material required for girl of eight years, 4½ yards, 27 inches wide; 2¼ yards, 44 inches; 2 yards, 50 inches.

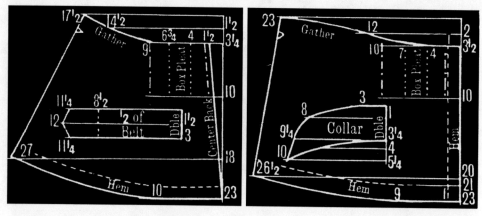

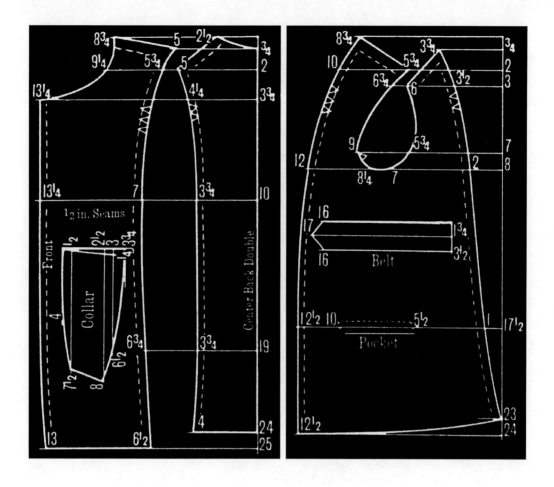

BOYS' SUIT.

A very pretty Knickerbocker suit for boys with Norfolk jacket is provided for by the diagrams given on this page and the page following. A peculiarity of the jacket is that the sides are cut in a single piece, the seams coming over the shoulder under the applied straps or pleats. A diagram for the straps is given, in two lengths, for the back and the front. These straps are to be folded under on each edge until the edges meet. They are to be stitched ¼ inch from each edge, leaving an opening at waist for the belt to pass under. A diagram for one half of the belt is given.

Draft by general instructions.

Material required for boy of eight years, for jacket, 2½ yards, 27 inches wide; 1½ yards, 50 inches.

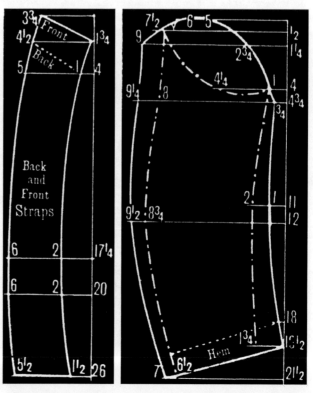

63

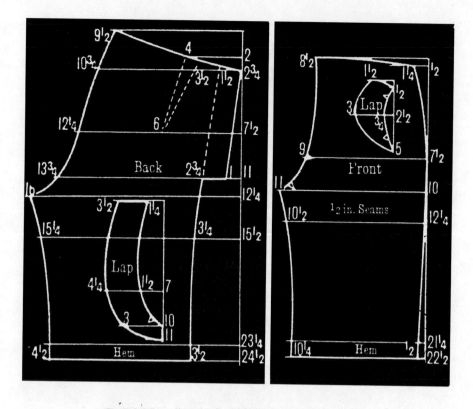

BOYS' KNICKERBOCKERS.

The diagram above is for knickerbockers for boys. Knickerbockers are now most generally used for boys rather than the fitted knee trousers. They are more comfortable and practical looking, and, best of all, are far more easily made. Material used in the ready-made clothing for boys is generally very inferior to that used for men. So if the boys' suit is made from some cast-off garment of larger size it is generally far more durable than the shop-made garment. This is an argument for home work.

If a long closing is made, as for men, use the pattern for the long "lap" or fly. If made otherwise, use the pattern for the short "lap." The bottom may be finished with a hem for a casing for an elastic or draw-string, or may be gathered into a band and buttoned.

Amount of material required for boy of eight years, 1½ yards, 27 inches wide; ¾ yard, 50 inches.

DUTCH BONNET.

A child's Dutch bonnet pattern may be made from the adjoining diagrams. It may be trimmed in any way to suit the taste. It may be made of lace, of all-over embroidery, or any material desired.

Draft by scale corresponding with a measurement taken around the fullest part of the head.

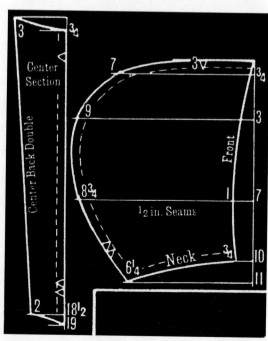